P9-DDZ-269

0206676

"Segregation and democracy are incompatible; blacks should maintain the struggle for equal rights while accepting the responsibilities that come with freedom; whites must demonstrate that democracy is color-blind."

—RALPH BUNCHE

RALPH BUNCHE

BY JOSEPH D. MCNAIR

COVER PHOTO

Portrait of Ralph Bunche
Courtesy of the United Nations

Published in the United States of America by The Child's World®, Inc.
PO Box 326
Chanhassen, MN 55317-0326
800-599-READ
www.childsworld.com

Product Manager Mary Francis-DeMarois/The Creative Spark
Designer Robert E. Bonaker/Graphic Design & Consulting Co.
Editorial Direction Elizabeth Sirimarco Budd
Contributors Mary Berendes, Red Line Editorial, Katherine Stevenson, Ph.D.

Library of Congress Cataloging-in-Publication Data
McNair, Joseph D.
Ralph Bunche / by Joseph D. McNair.
p. cm.
Includes bibliographical references (p.   ) and index.
ISBN 1-56766-922-0 (library bound : alk. paper)
1. Bunche, Ralph J. (Ralph Johnson), 1904–1971—Juvenile literature.
2. Statesmen—United States—Biography—Juvenile literature. 3. African
Americans—Biography—Juvenile literature. 4. United Nations—Biography—Juvenile
literature. 5. Nobel Prizes—Biography—Juvenile literature. [1. Bunche, Ralph J.
(Ralph Johnson), 1904–1971. 2. Statesmen. 3. African Americans—Biography.
4. Nobel Prizes—Biography.]   I. Title.
E748.B885 M43 2001
973'.0496073'0092—dc21

2001001075

Contents

©David Lees/CORBIS

RALPH JOHNSON BUNCHE WAS AN AMERICAN LEADER
AND GOVERNMENT ADVISOR. HE IS MOST FAMOUS FOR
HIS WORK WITH THE UNITED NATIONS, IN WHICH HE
HELPED BRING PEACE TO THE JEWS AND ARABS IN
PALESTINE. FOR HIS EFFORTS, BUNCHE WON THE
NOBEL PEACE PRIZE IN 1950.

The Peacemaker

It was the end of World War II. During the war, German leader Adolf Hitler had attempted to kill the Jewish people of Germany and several other European nations. He had Jews captured and herded onto railroad cars that took them to concentration camps. Millions were killed in the camps. Others died of starvation, disease, and sorrow.

Some Jews escaped Germany, fleeing from their homeland. But many had trouble finding a place to go. Some countries would not allow Jews to enter, even though officials knew turning them away endangered the **refugees'** lives. For the refugees, these were dark, terrible times.

European Jews longed for their own homeland, a safe haven. Many Jews believed they should return to the place in the Middle East where their ancestors had lived, the land around the holy city of Jerusalem. This land was called Palestine.

But Palestine already had its own Arab people whose families had lived there for almost 4,000 years. Time after time, Palestine's Arabs had lost control of their land to outsiders—Assyrians, Babylonians, Persians, Romans, Muslims, and Turks. Since the end of World War I in 1918, Great Britain had ruled Palestine.

The British had already promised the Palestinians that one day they would have their independence and rule their own land. But the British had also promised European Jews that they would have a homeland in Palestine.

When World War II ended, many Jews went to Palestine, expecting Great Britain's promise to be kept. Trouble followed, however. Jews and Palestinians fought over the land and over the holy city of Jerusalem. Both Jews and Palestinians truly believed they had a right to Palestine's land.

A new international organization was formed to keep peace in the region as well as in other parts of the world. Members of the United Nations (UN) came from countries all over the world. Britain handed over the rule of Palestine to the UN, which sent **representatives** to talk to people there. The UN representatives decided that Arabs and Jews could not be expected to live together. In 1947, the UN split Palestine into three parts: an Arab state, a Jewish state, and a small international zone surrounding Jerusalem.

But the UN decision did not solve the problem. Arabs and Jews continued to fight. The British left Palestine in May of 1948. Then the Jews declared their section of Palestine to be a new nation called Israel. The region's Arab nations did not accept this declaration. They sent soldiers to attack Israel. The Arab-Israeli War had begun.

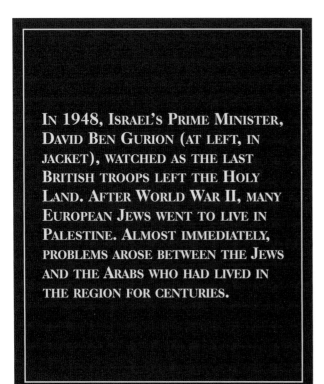

IN 1948, ISRAEL'S PRIME MINISTER, DAVID BEN GURION (AT LEFT, IN JACKET), WATCHED AS THE LAST BRITISH TROOPS LEFT THE HOLY LAND. AFTER WORLD WAR II, MANY EUROPEAN JEWS WENT TO LIVE IN PALESTINE. ALMOST IMMEDIATELY, PROBLEMS AROSE BETWEEN THE JEWS AND THE ARABS WHO HAD LIVED IN THE REGION FOR CENTURIES.

©Bettmann/CORBIS

©Jerry Cooke/CORBIS

The United Nations tried to bring peace to the Middle East, but without success. By the spring of 1948, a war had begun between the region's Arabs and Jews. Here young Israeli soldiers guard their border during the Arab-Israeli war.

The UN arranged a **cease-fire,** but it did not seem as if peace would last. The UN then sent a **mediator** to Jerusalem. The mediator, Count Folke Bernadotte of Sweden, talked to both sides and tried to stop another war from breaking out. But Bernadotte was **assassinated** in September of 1948. Suddenly, the UN needed a new mediator. Who could they turn to? Who could handle such a delicate and dangerous situation? To UN officials, the choice was obvious: Bernadotte's assistant, Ralph Bunche.

And a good choice it was. No one could understand the problems of Palestine better than Bunche, an African American from Detroit, Michigan. Raised in poverty, he knew first hand about conflict. For years, he had used his brilliant mind to study the world's biggest problems. He had been involved with the United Nations since its very beginning.

Bunche worked to gain the trust of both sides. When war broke out again, he **negotiated** with representatives on both sides for seven long weeks. Many times he felt like quitting—but quitting was never really an option. In a letter to his wife, he said, "I talk, argue, coax and threaten these stubborn people day and night. I make a bit of progress here and another bit there, but it's so slow and **arduous.** Sometimes I feel like I should just tell them to go home."

But Bunche kept his eye on the prize. On February 24, 1949, thanks to his efforts, the two sides agreed to an **armistice.** The Jews called his efforts superhuman. The Arabs said he was one of the greatest men in the world. No one else would bring these two groups to **compromise** for the next 20 years.

For his efforts, on December 10, 1950, Bunche was awarded the Nobel Peace Prize—the first black man ever to receive this great honor.

©Bettmann/Corbis

ARAB AND ISRAELI LEADERS ARE SHOWN HERE SIGNING AN ARMISTICE THAT ENDED THE WAR. FACING THE CAMERA IS RALPH BUNCHE (AT THE TABLE, FAR LEFT), WITH HIS AIDES FROM THE UN MEDIATION GROUP.

A Proud Family

Ralph Johnson Bunche was born on August 7, 1904, in Detroit, Michigan. Ralph's parents were Fred Bunche and Olive Johnson Bunche. Fred Bunche was from Zanesville, Ohio. He was a handsome, dashing man who loved music.

Fred was working for a traveling circus when he met Olive Johnson. She was the second child of Thomas and Lucy Taylor Johnson. Her grandfather, James Johnson, was free during the time of slavery. He was a farmer who owned land, unlike most black people at the time. James's wife, Eleanor, was a freed slave. Their son Thomas, Olive's father, eventually went to college, an unusual achievement for a black man of the day. Thomas then became a teacher at a school for freed slaves. Thomas met his future wife, Lucy Taylor, when she was one of his students.

Thomas and Lucy had a happy marriage, but it ended far too early. Thomas Johnson died at the age of 40, leaving 35-year-old Lucy as the head of her household. She took this responsibility seriously. Lucy had five children and no money to support them. She moved her family several times, looking for work and a safe place to live. They finally settled in Detroit, Michigan, where Lucy's daughter Olive would later meet Fred Bunche.

After a short romance, Olive and Fred Bunche married. Ralph was their first child. Later they had a daughter named Grace. Olive and Fred could not afford their own house, so they lived with Lucy. Grandma Lucy would always play an important role in Ralph's life.

Ralph and his family lived in Detroit until he was almost 11 years old. He loved the city. In the winter, he hitched his sled behind wagons to catch a fast ride down snowy streets. In the summer, he and his friends swam in the river. Walking home from school, he enjoyed listening to street bands along the way.

Detroit History

RALPH JOHNSON BUNCHE WAS BORN IN THIS HOUSE IN DETROIT, MICHIGAN. THERE IS SOME QUESTION ABOUT THE DATE OF HIS BIRTH. MOST SOURCES LIST HIS BIRTH YEAR AS 1904, BUT HIS SCHOOL RECORDS LIST IT AS 1903. FAMILY MEMBERS SAY HIS ORIGINAL BIRTH CERTIFICATE WAS LOST. WHEN A NEW ONE WAS ISSUED IN 1940, HIS AUNT RECORDED HIS BIRTH DATE AS 1904. THAT YEAR IS THE ONE MOST OFTEN USED IN BOOKS AND ARTICLES ABOUT HIM.

R alph was a good student as well. He had to be, because Grandma Lucy, whom he called Nana, was serious about education.

In 1914, both Olive and her brother Charlie got tuberculosis, a disease that affects the lungs. Hoping fresh, dry air would help them recover, Lucy moved the family to Albuquerque, New Mexico. Fred Bunche stayed in Detroit for a short time and then moved to Albuquerque as well.

Young Ralph liked Albuquerque. He and his Uncle Charlie had fun together hunting jack rabbits on the outskirts of town. Ralph was one of two black children who attended the local one-room school. In 1916, Fred Bunche left Albuquerque to look for work. The family never saw him again. Shortly after he left, Olive died of tuberculosis. Not long after, Ralph's Uncle Charlie died as well.

RALPH'S PARENTS WERE OLIVE AND FRED BUNCHE, SHOWN AT RIGHT.

Library of Congress

Library of Congress

Library of Congress

The deaths of Lucy's two grown children were difficult for her to bear. But she put this grief behind her and focused on raising Ralph and his sister. Grandma Lucy passed on her own values to the children. She felt proud of who she was and where she came from. In a time when many African Americans were ashamed of their color and culture, Ralph Bunche's Nana was the proudest black woman around! She taught her children and grand-children that it was good to be black.

She taught Ralph to respect himself and to act with dignity. She told him he should never pick a fight. But she also told him he must never run away from one if an important principle was involved. She told Ralph that he could achieve anything a white person could. She told her family to be proud of their race.

After the deaths of Olive and Charlie, there was no reason for the family to stay in Albuquerque. Lucy decided they should move even farther west. She and her two grandchildren packed their bags and moved to Los Angeles, California. They settled there in April of 1917.

RALPH, SHOWN HERE WITH HIS SISTER GRACE, WAS AN EXCELLENT STUDENT. HIS GRANDMA LUCY EXPECTED A GREAT DEAL OF HIM, AND HE WAS EAGER TO MAKE HER PROUD.

Library of Congress

LUCY JOHNSON, RALPH'S
GRANDMOTHER, IS SHOWN
HERE AS A YOUNG WOMAN.
THROUGHOUT RALPH'S LIFE,
LUCY WAS AN IMPORTANT
INFLUENCE. SHE INSISTED
THAT HE DO THE VERY BEST
HE COULD AT ANYTHING HE
TRIED. SHE MADE HIM FEEL
PROUD OF WHO HE WAS.

Ralph enrolled at the Thirtieth Street Intermediate School. Almost all the school's students were white. Nana watched his progress closely. She was concerned when he didn't show as much interest in his studies as he had in Detroit and Albuquerque. When she went to see the principal, she found out that Ralph was taking mainly **vocational** classes. Vocational classes teach trade skills such as woodworking rather than academic subjects such as mathematics. The teachers at the Thirtieth Street School believed vocational classes were the best choice for black children. Nana insisted they immediately let Ralph study subjects that would prepare him for college. Ralph, she told the school's principal, was definitely going to college.

In 1919, Ralph enrolled in Jefferson High School, which also had mostly white students. He excelled in basketball. He was also one of the top students in his class. Even so, he was denied membership to an honor society because he was black. When he graduated in 1921, he was the **valedictorian,** which meant he had earned the highest grades of any student in his class.

University of California-Los Angeles

RALPH WAS NOT ONLY A GOOD STUDENT, BUT AN EXCELLENT ATHLETE AS WELL. HE PLAYED BASKETBALL IN BOTH HIGH SCHOOL AND COLLEGE.

In 1922, Ralph enrolled at the University of California at Los Angeles (UCLA). The school gave him an athletic **scholarship** to help pay his expenses. Ralph's college days were filled with success. He was popular with students and teachers. He joined the debate team, wrote for the campus newspaper, and was a star on the basketball team. Ralph also organized discussions between the school's black and white students about race and other issues. He did all of this and still worked part time to earn spending money. Ralph Bunche wasn't too proud to work—and to work hard.

Ralph was also an excellent student who earned high grades at UCLA. He majored in **political science.** He especially liked learning about world affairs. He studied **colonialism,** a policy many powerful nations had. Countries that practiced colonialism took over other territories and then governed them. The United States had once been a set of colonies belonging to Great Britain. The American colonies won their independence in the Revolutionary War. In his college classes, Ralph learned about many other colonies that still existed. European countries such as England and France still controlled huge parts of Africa, Asia, and Central and South America. The European rulers often took power from native peoples who lived in these places.

Ralph graduated from UCLA in 1927. Once again, he was the class valedictorian. He decided to continue his education and was pleased when he got the chance to study at Harvard University, one of the best schools in the country.

Corbis

WHEN RALPH GRADUATED FROM UCLA IN 1927, HE WAS ONCE AGAIN VALEDICTORIAN OF HIS CLASS. HE WENT ON TO CONTINUE HIS STUDIES AT HARVARD UNIVERSITY, SHOWN ABOVE.

University of California at Los Angeles

AFTER GRADUATING FROM UCLA, BUNCHE WAS ONE OF 40 AFRICAN AMERICANS WHO ENROLLED AT HARVARD UNIVERSITY IN 1927.

Diplomat in the Making

Ralph Bunche received his **master's degree** in political science from Harvard University in 1928. He was then offered a job at Howard University and began teaching in its political science department. He would teach at Howard, sometimes on a part-time basis, until 1941.

On June 23, 1930, Bunche married Ruth Ethel Harris. The couple met during Bunche's first year at Howard. While teaching, Ralph continued his graduate education. He studied for a **doctoral degree** from Harvard. Bunche decided to write his **dissertation** about colonialism. To research the topic, he traveled to France and England as well as to the African nations of Dahomey, Togo, Senegal, and Liberia. During these travels, Bunche gathered information about colonies and the governments that controlled them. In February of 1934, he received his doctoral degree from Harvard. He was the first African American to earn a doctorate in political science from a U.S. university.

He also won an important prize for the best dissertation in the country that year.

After he received his degree, Bunche continued his studies. Through his travels, he had come to see the world differently from most people. He was disturbed by the effects of colonialism, which he believed created racial **prejudice** by giving one race power over another. He also believed that colonialism created a lack of opportunity for those who had no power. He vowed to oppose these forces in any way he could. In his view, colonialism would have to come to an end. He wanted to help colonies become self-governing nations—without bloodshed.

During his career, Bunche would help people all over the world as a **diplomat** and peacemaker. He was also interested in what was going on in his own country. He especially wanted to see better treatment for African Americans.

Bunche hated the **segregation** practices that kept African Americans separated from whites. In many areas of the United States, segregation policies forced black children to go to separate schools. The policies also banned blacks from using the same libraries, playing at the same parks, and eating at the same restaurants as white Americans. Bunche believed all citizens of the United States should have the same **civil rights,** regardless of race.

Bunche participated in many civil rights **protests.** In 1935, he and a civil rights leader named John Davis organized a conference at Howard University. Leading African American intellectuals gathered to talk about the plight of African Americans. That same year, Bunche joined with other leaders to found the National Negro Congress. The aim of this organization was to provide better education and opportunities for blacks in the United States.

As he thought about affairs in the United States, Ralph Bunche also continued to learn about Africa and African issues. On a trip with his family to London, Bunche met African leaders from Uganda and the Gold Coast (now Ghana).

University of California-Los Angeles

In 1934, Ralph Bunche became the first African American to earn a doctoral degree in political science from a U.S. university. He earned the degree from Harvard University in Cambridge, Massachusetts.

After his wife and daughters returned to the United States, Bunche went on to Africa alone. He toured South Africa and learned firsthand about its segregated society. He also visited Kenya, the Congo, and Uganda.

All over Africa, he saw racial prejudice. In Africa's European colonies, white government officials still controlled the land. They often deprived native Africans of basic rights.

Bettmann/Corbis

DURING HIS TRAVELS IN AFRICA, BUNCHE SAW HOW NATIVE AFRICANS LIVED. WHITE EUROPEANS HAD CONTROLLED MANY PARTS OF THE CONTINENT FOR CENTURIES. IN SOUTH AFRICA, FOR EXAMPLE, NATIVE AFRICANS WERE SEGREGATED FROM WHITE SOCIETY. THE NATIVES WERE FORCED TO LIVE IN IMPOVERISHED SHANTYTOWNS, LIKE THE ONE SHOWN HERE, AND HAD NO CONTROL OVER THEIR GOVERNMENT. BUNCHE BELIEVED THAT THIS WAS VERY WRONG.

In 1938, Bunche went on to Asia, where he visited Singapore, Bali, Hong Kong, and the Philippines—all European or American colonies. Everywhere he went, Bunche took photographs and wrote volumes of notes. Later that year, he began working with another **scholar,** Gunnar Myrdal from Sweden. Together the two men began a detailed study of black people in the United States. Myrdal, with Bunche's help, wrote a book called *An American Dilemma: The Negro Problem and Modern Democracy.* It was the largest study anyone had made of race relations in the United States.

By the 1940s, Ralph Bunche was widely recognized as the most knowledgeable American scholar studying Africa and the African people. Because of this, the U.S. government asked for his help when World War II began. In 1941, he went to work for the government's Office of Strategic Services (OSS), which later became the Central Intelligence Agency (CIA). At the time Bunche joined, the OSS included scholars and journalists who worked together collecting information about the war. In that stage of the war, Great Britain, France, and the Soviet Union were fighting Germany. The United States joined the war later that year after Japan, Germany's **ally,** attacked Pearl Harbor in Hawaii.

In the OSS, Bunche was the expert on African affairs. He wrote reports for the army on what fighting would be like in Africa. He also worked to convince African Americans that the United States should be fighting in the war. He pushed employers to hire African Americans to work in factories that produced supplies for the military.

In 1944, Bunche accepted a position at the State Department, which is in charge of the nation's relations with other countries. He again focused on Africa and colonial issues. He was the first African American to run a department in the federal government.

THE JAPANESE ATTACKED PEARL HARBOR (ABOVE) ON DECEMBER 7, 1941, AND THE UNITED STATES ENTERED WORLD WAR II THE FOLLOWING DAY. DURING THE WAR, BUNCHE WORKED FOR THE GOVERNMENT'S OFFICE OF STRATEGIC SERVICES (OSS), WHICH LATER BECAME THE CENTRAL INTELLIGENCE AGENCY.

Soon Bunche's role in world affairs became even more important. In 1945, World War II finally ended. The war had taken a terrible toll on countries all over the world. Years earlier, after World War I, many nations had joined together to form the League of Nations. The League's aim was to work for world peace. But during World War II, leaders had begun to discuss replacing the old League of Nations with a new organization: the United Nations.

Fifty countries established the UN. Bunche was among the representatives who met to determine its goals. He helped write the UN's **charter.** On June 26, 1945, the new United Nations Charter was signed at the Conference on International Organizations in San Francisco. Bunche won great respect from everyone involved in the process.

Corbis

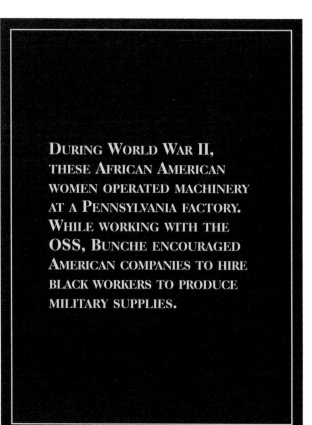

DURING WORLD WAR II, THESE AFRICAN AMERICAN WOMEN OPERATED MACHINERY AT A PENNSYLVANIA FACTORY. WHILE WORKING WITH THE OSS, BUNCHE ENCOURAGED AMERICAN COMPANIES TO HIRE BLACK WORKERS TO PRODUCE MILITARY SUPPLIES.

Bettmann/Corbis

ON JUNE 26, 1945, THE NEW UNITED NATIONS CHARTER WAS SIGNED BY
WORLD LEADERS AT THE CONFERENCE ON INTERNATIONAL ORGANIZATIONS IN
SAN FRANCISCO. BUNCHE HAD CONTRIBUTED HIS TALENT TO THE WRITING OF
THIS IMPORTANT DOCUMENT.

The United Nations

Ralph Bunche would remain involved in the United Nations for decades. After the charter went into effect, Bunche was **appointed** to be a representative to the UN General Assembly. He attended its first meeting in London in January of 1946. There the General Assembly made important decisions. It appointed Trygve Lie (pronounced TRIG-vee LEE) of Norway as the UN's secretary general. It also selected New York as the site for the UN headquarters.

Bunche spent 1946 taking part in the General Assembly as well as working for the State Department. On April 22, 1947, he resigned from the State Department so he could work full time for the UN. One of the UN's long-term goals was to help colonies all over the world gain independence. Bunche's input would be very important.

Trygve Lie asked that Bunche be appointed director of the Trusteeship Council. This council looked after former colonies that were in trusteeship, meaning that they were preparing to become independent nations. Most of these lands were in Africa. Bunche's job was especially important because in the early days of the UN, few members of the General Assembly were Africans. Countries with colonies in Africa seldom appointed natives to be UN representatives.

In May of 1947, Bunche took on added responsibilities. He was appointed to a special committee formed to gather information about the situation in Palestine. Bunche went to Palestine and then wrote most of the committee's report to the UN General Assembly. It was this report that convinced members to divide Palestine between the Arabs and the Jews.

A year later, Bunche took a new special assignment. He became the assistant to Count Bernadotte, the UN mediator trying to bring peace to the Middle East. When Bernadotte was assassinated, it was Bunche who took over his duties.

RALPH BUNCHE (LEFT) LOOKS AT A MAP OF THE MIDDLE EAST WITH ANOTHER UN OFFICIAL. IN MAY OF 1947, BUNCHE WAS ASSIGNED TO A SPECIAL COMMITTEE CHARGED WITH STUDYING THE PROBLEMS IN PALESTINE.

Bettmann/Corbis

HERE WRECKAGE IS CLEARED FROM BEN YEHUDA STREET IN ISRAEL FOLLOWING AN EXPLOSION DURING THE ARAB-ISRAELI WAR. THIS EVENT ALONE KILLED 52 PEOPLE AND INJURED AT LEAST 100 MORE. SUCH TRAGEDIES PROMPTED THE UNITED NATIONS TO WORK TO RESOLVE THE CRISIS. IT WAS RALPH BUNCHE'S SKILL THAT HELPED ARABS AND ISRAELIS REACH AN AGREEMENT.

As the UN mediator, Bunche negotiated an armistice between Egypt and Israel, and then another armistice between Israel and Jordan. In April of 1949, he returned home to a hero's welcome in the United States. President Harry Truman praised him as a superb diplomat. Truman asked Bunche to become assistant secretary of state for Near Eastern, South Asian, and African affairs. Bunche turned the offer down because he did not want his family to move back to Washington, D.C. Segregation was still a fact of life in the nation's capital, and he did not want his family to live under those conditions. Instead, Bunche decided to continue working for the UN in New York City, where **discrimination** was less of a problem. He returned to his position as head of the Trusteeship Council.

On July 17, 1949, Bunche received an important award from the National Association for the Advancement of Colored People (NAACP). This organization awarded him its Spingarn Medal for the highest or noblest achievement by an African American.

The following year, Bunche received an even greater honor. In December of 1950, he was awarded the Nobel Peace Prize. Every year the Nobel Foundation awards this prize to the person who has done the most to bring about world peace. After he received this prize, Bunche received awards from many colleges and universities. He was also offered many teaching jobs, one of which he accepted. He became a professor of government at Harvard but still continued his work with the United Nations.

On January 1, 1955, Bunche became the UN's undersecretary for special political affairs. Dag Hammarskjöld (pronounced DAHG HA-mur-shuld), from Sweden, was the new secretary general. Hammarskjöld assigned Bunche to deal with specific problems. One of Bunche's first assignments was to study peaceful uses for **atomic energy,** such as creating electricity. Then, in 1956, Bunche helped end another war in the Middle East. The war started when Israel, France, and Great Britain attacked Egypt, after Egypt took over the Suez Canal. The following year, Bunche enjoyed a trip to Ghana, which was celebrating its independence.

In 1960, Bunche undertook a very difficult and dangerous task. The Congo had just become an independent nation, and many different groups were fighting for control of the new government. The country's president had been kidnapped and killed. Bunche went to the Congo with UN troops to bring peace to the country. It took a very long time to achieve this. For three years, Bunche struggled with this conflict. While Bunche was in the Congo, Dag Hammarskjöld died in a plane crash. Hammarskjöld's replacement, U Thant (pronounced OO THAHNT) from Burma, asked Bunche to continue his work.

In the years that followed, Bunche acted as a peacemaker in the countries of Yemen, Cyprus, and Vietnam. In 1963, President John Kennedy selected Bunche to receive the Presidential Medal of Freedom. This award honors American citizens who have worked for national security and world peace.

Bettmann/Corbis

IN 1957, BUNCHE AND OTHER OFFICIALS FLEW TO THE COUNTRY OF GHANA TO ATTEND THE CELEBRATION MARKING THAT COUNTRY'S INDEPENDENCE FROM GREAT BRITAIN. SHOWN HERE (LEFT TO RIGHT) ARE RICHARD L. JONES, U.S. AMBASSADOR TO LIBERIA; RALPH BUNCHE; AND CONGRESSMAN ADAM CLAYTON POWELL.

When Bunche was in the United States, he took part in the Civil Rights Movement, continuing to fight for equality for African Americans. With the Reverend Martin Luther King Jr., Bunche led the 1965 civil rights march in Montgomery, Alabama. Three years later, in 1968, he was named the UN's undersecretary general. He was second in charge of the United Nations—a great honor in recognition of all he had done for the organization.

Bettmann/Corbis

BUNCHE PARTICIPATED IN PROTESTS DURING THE CIVIL RIGHTS MOVEMENT. HERE HE IS SHOWN (WALKING IN FRONT CENTER) LEADING A 1965 MARCH WITH MARTIN LUTHER KING JR. IN ALABAMA.

Corbis

FLAGS OF THE MEMBER NATIONS FLY IN FRONT OF THE UNITED NATIONS HEADQUARTERS IN NEW YORK CITY. RALPH BUNCHE WORKED FULL TIME FOR THE UNITED NATIONS FOR NEARLY 25 YEARS, FROM 1947 UNTIL HIS RETIREMENT IN 1970.

In 1970 Bunche retired from the UN after a long and distinguished career. He died peacefully on December 9, 1971, at the age of 67. His death made headlines all over the world. Every member of the UN's General Assembly stood in silence to honor his memory.

Ralph Bunche was a scholar and an intellectual, a political **activist,** and an international leader. He fought for the rights and dreams of African Americans and of people everywhere in the world.

Bunche saw the similarities between what was happening to African Americans at home and what was happening to people in colonies in Africa, Asia, and Central and South America. In all these places, including the United States, people in power were depriving others of their rights.

Bunche fought this system of injustice. He worked to end colonialism and racial prejudice. And he worked to bring peace.

Bunche may be most famous for his work with the United Nations to bring peace to the troubled Middle East. But this is far from his only achievement. He was a man who believed in the potential of human beings to live in peace. And he did what he could to help the world reach that goal.

RALPH BUNCHE DIED IN 1971 AFTER A LIFETIME OF SERVICE TO HIS COUNTRY— AND TO THE WORLD.

Timeline

1904	Ralph Johnson Bunche is born on August 7 in Detroit, Michigan.
1914	Bunche's grandmother, Lucy Taylor Johnson, moves her family to Albuquerque, New Mexico, where Ralph attends elementary school.
1916	Fred Bunche leaves Albuquerque to look for work and never returns.
1917	Ralph's mother dies. He and his sister Grace move to Los Angeles with their grandmother.
1921	Bunche graduates from Jefferson High School as the class valedictorian.
1922	Bunche receives an athletic scholarship to attend the University of California at Los Angeles (UCLA).
1927	Bunche graduates from UCLA as valedictorian.
1928	After earning a master's degree in political science from Harvard University, Bunche becomes an instructor in political science and government at Howard University.
1930	Bunche marries Ruth Ethel Harris.
1931	Bunche studies French colonialism in the African regions of Dahomey and Togo.
1934	When he receives his doctoral degree from Harvard, Bunche becomes the first African American to earn a doctorate in political science from a U.S. university.
1935	Bunche helps found the National Negro Congress.
1938	Bunche works with Swedish scholar Gunnar Myrdal, who publishes a respected book on U.S. race relations several years later.
1941	Bunche joins the Office of Strategic Services as its expert in African affairs.
1944	Bunche accepts a position at the State Department. He also helps create the United Nations Charter, which defines the organization's goals.
1945	The United Nations Charter is signed on June 26.
1946	In January, Bunche becomes a representative to the UN's first General Assembly while continuing to work for the State Department.
1947	Bunche is appointed to the United Nations Special Committee on Palestine.
1948	The Secretary General names Bunche the assistant to the UN's mediator, Count Folke Bernadotte. In September, Bernadotte is assassinated, and Bunche is asked to take over the position of mediator.
1949	Bunche negotiates armistices between Israel and Arab nations and returns home to a hero's welcome in New York City. On July 17, the NAACP awards Bunche its Spingarn Medal.
1950	In December, Bunche is awarded the Nobel Peace Prize. He becomes a professor of government at Harvard.
1955	On January 1, Bunche is named UN undersecretary for special political affairs.
1956	Bunche helps end a war in Egypt.
1960	Bunche travels to the Congo to attempt to stop fighting between groups trying to gain control of the new nation's government.
1963	President John Kennedy awards Bunche the Presidential Medal of Freedom.
1970	Bunche retires from the United Nations after nearly 25 years of service.
1971	At 67 years of age, Ralph Bunche dies on December 9.

Glossary

activist (AK-tiv-ist)
An activist is someone who takes strong action to support a view or belief. Bunche was a political activist.

ally (AL-lye)
An ally is a nation or person who agrees to help another. Japan was an ally of Germany during World War II.

appointed (uh-POYNT-ed)
When someone is appointed to a position, he or she is officially chosen and asked to accept. Bunche was appointed to several positions with the United Nations.

arduous (ARD-joo-uss)
If something is arduous, it is difficult and requires much effort. Bunche said his work in the Middle East was "slow and arduous."

armistice (ARM-iss-tiss)
An armistice is a temporary end to warfare. In 1949, Bunche helped bring about an armistice between Arab nations and Israel.

assassinated (uh-SASS-ih-nayt-ed)
When an important or famous person has been murdered, he or she has been assassinated. Count Folke Bernadotte, a UN mediator, was assassinated in 1948.

atomic energy (uh-TOM-ik EN-er-jee)
Atomic energy is a kind of energy produced by pushing atoms together or splitting them apart. Bunche was asked to study peaceful uses for atomic energy.

cease-fire (SEES FIRE)
In war, a cease-fire is a time during which both sides stop fighting. The UN arranged a cease-fire between Arab and Israeli soldiers.

charter (CHAR-ter)
A charter is an official written document that defines the principles and goals of an organization. Bunche helped write the charter of the United Nations.

civil rights (SIV-el RYTZ)
Civil rights are a person's rights to freedom and equal treatment. Bunche believed that all U.S. citizens should have the same civil rights, regardless of race.

colonialism (kuh-LOH-nee-ul-iz-im)
Colonialism is a practice in which one country takes over and controls another region. Bunche believed that colonialism led to racial prejudice because it gave one race control over another.

compromise (KOM-pruh-mize)
A compromise is a way to settle a disagreement in which both sides give up part of what they want. Bunche convinced Arabs and Israelis to compromise.

diplomat (DIP-loh-mat)
A diplomat is someone who speaks for a country in discussions with other countries. President Harry Truman praised Bunche as a superb diplomat.

discrimination (dis-krim-ih-NAY-shun)
Discrimination is the unfair treatment of people simply because they are different. Bunche did not want his family to face discrimination.

dissertation (diss-ser-TAY-shun)
A dissertation is a long paper a student writes to earn a doctoral degree. Bunche wrote his dissertation on colonialism.

Glossary

doctoral degree (DOK-tor-ull deh-GREE)
A doctoral degree is the highest degree a college or a university gives to students. To earn a doctoral degree, a person studies for many years and then writes a dissertation.

master's degree (MAS-terz deh-GREE)
A master's degree is an advanced degree earned after graduating from college. Bunche earned a master's degree in political science from Harvard University.

mediator (MEE-dee-ay-tor)
A mediator is a person who helps settle a disagreement between two people or sides. The United Nations sent a mediator to solve problems between Israel and neighboring Arab nations.

negotiate (neh-GOH-shee-ate)
When people negotiate, they talk about a difference and try to come to an agreement. Bunche helped negotiate an end to war between Israel and its Arab neighbors.

political science (poh-LIH-tih-kull SY-enss)
Political science is the study of how governments are run. Bunche earned degrees in political science.

prejudice (PREH-juh-diss)
Prejudice is a negative feeling or opinion about someone without a good reason. Bunche believed that colonialism created racial prejudice.

protests (PROH-tests)
Protests are public statements or gatherings in which people speak out to say something is wrong. During the Civil Rights Movement, Americans attended protests to speak out against the poor treatment of minorities.

refugees (reh-fyoo-JEEZ)
Refugees are people who flee to a foreign country to escape danger or persecution. During World War II, some countries would not help Jewish refugees.

representatives (rep-reh-ZEN-tuh-tivz)
Representatives are people asked to speak or act for others. The United Nations sent representatives to Palestine.

scholar (SKOL-er)
A scholar is a learned person who has done advanced studies in a field. Ralph Bunche was a scholar.

scholarship (SKOL-er-ship)
A scholarship is money awarded to a student to help pay for his or her education. Bunche earned a scholarship to attend the University of California at Los Angeles (UCLA).

segregation (seh-greh-GAY-shun)
Segregation is a policy of keeping people apart. For many years, segregation laws separated blacks and whites in parts of the United States.

valedictorian (val-eh-dik-TOR-ee-un)
A valedictorian is the student with the highest rank in his or her graduating class. Bunche was valedictorian of his class both in high school and in college.

vocational (voh-KAY-shun-ull)
A vocational class teaches students a trade or skill that will help them find a job. Bunche's grandmother was unhappy to learn that he had been placed in vocational classes rather than academic classes.

Index

Further Information

Books and Magazines

Keene, Ann T. *Peacemakers: Winners of the Nobel Peace Prize* (Oxford Profiles).
New York: Oxford University Press, 1999.

McKissack, Pat, and Fred McKissack. *Ralph J. Bunche: Peacemaker* (Great African
Americans). Springfield, NJ: Enslow Publishers, 2001.

Ross, Stewart. *Causes and Consequences of the Arab-Israeli Conflict* (Causes and
Consequences). Austin, TX: Raintree/Steck Vaughn, 1995.

Stein, R. Conrad. *The United Nations* (Cornerstones of Freedom). Chicago:
Childrens Press, 1994.

Web Sites

Learn more about Ralph Bunche:
http://www.pbs.org/ralphbunche/
http://ralphbunchegl.virtualave.net/drralph.htm

Learn more about the Nobel Peace Prize:
http://www.nobel.se/peace/

Read the speech given at the Nobel ceremony in honor of Ralph Bunche:
http://www.nobel.se/peace/laureates/1950/index.html

Visit the official site of the United Nations:
http://www.un.org/

Read quotations from Ralph Bunche:
http://www.bemorecreative.com/one/895.htm